COLLECTED CURIOSITIES

POEMS, ESSAYS, & OPINIONS

KATHLEEN M. JACOBS

Jan-Carol
Publishing, Inc

Collected Curiosities
Poems, Essays, & Opinions
Kathleen M. Jacobs

First Edition Published August 2017
Little Creek Books
Imprint of Jan-Carol Publishing, Inc.
Cover Design: Anna Hartman

ISBN: 978-1-945619-35-9

You may contact the publisher:
Jan-Carol Publishing, Inc.
PO Box 701
Johnson City, TN 37605
publisher@jancarolpublishing.com
jancarolpublishing.com

For John

Also by Kathleen M. Jacobs

Honeysuckle Holiday
Marble Town

Collected Curiosities

Poems, Essays, & Opinions

ACKNOWLEDGMENTS

My earliest recollections of rich storytelling resonated from the soulful voice of Lila Spencer, a resolute matriarch of a large southern family during my childhood in Memphis, Tennessee. Coupled with her deep, convincing voice were also the mild notes rendered by my great-aunt, Dora Roling and her deeply-affecting husband, Herman. These stories formed the base for my own storytelling. I'm grateful to each of these lovers of words for impressing upon me—without their even knowing—the treasures that the spoken and written words convey, deeper and more lasting than ever imaginable.

Anna Hartman, you are a treasure that seems to transcend words. Thank you for creating yet another cover design that left me challenged to acknowledge with words my gratitude.

Brian Hoskinson, my continued thanks for your patience and vision and passion for my work.

Janie Jessee, my erudite publisher, my continued gratitude.

John Jacobs, thank you for more than I'll ever be able to quantify.

"Like a bird that wanders from her nest,
So is a man who wanders from his home."

—Proverbs 27:8

THE STUDENTS

They saunter in, like cows grazing,
moving in slow, syncopated steps,
unsoiled spiral notebooks waiting
to be congested with logarithms,
historical facts & figures, and,
with a bit of Irish luck & cool creativity,
poetry that sings & dances & beckons
to be set
free,
alive to all the
crackling leaves, the cool winds, &
the expansiveness of the open fields
reaching
towards the hyacinthine sky.

Tales From the Writing Life

Out of the Mouths of Babes

BY KATHLEEN M. JACOBS

As my nieces and nephews journeyed from picture books to story-books to chapter books, it seemed as if what truly sealed their love of reading were middle-grade mainstays such as *Charlotte's Web*, *A Wrinkle in Time*, *Because of Winn-Dixie*, *The House on Mango Street* and particularly (my favorite) *To Kill a Mockingbird*. As their thirst for more great stories grew, a seed was planted and sprouted: I should write a book to encourage young readers to turn their love of reading into a lifelong adventure.

After completing my first novel, I called my 14-year-old niece to see if she would be interested in reviewing the work and giving me her opinion. She is a discerning reader with a candid nature and regard for nothing but the "absolute truth on absolutely everything."

She eagerly agreed to read the manuscript, point-ing out first that she was very busy with her friends and schoolwork, but that she would try to work me in, hoping to get back to me within a few weeks.

We agreed upon a reader's fee of $10 an hour, and I mailed the manuscript to her, along with a list of myriad questions to answer after she read the story. When she telephoned a few weeks later to discuss the work, I was thrilled that she gave it a thumbs up, but she had a few suggestions.

"In Chapter 5, you need to give a clearer description of the train station. In Chapter 8, you don't need to explain what's going on in the bar in so much detail. Remember, readers want to figure out certain things for themselves. And in Chapter 11, you need to provide more information, because I'm not sure what's going on. I do love the dialogue that goes on in the book between the characters, and I want to know if you're going to write a series, because I fell in love with all these people, even the dad, who I shouldn't have fallen in love with. And, oh, by the way, you misspelled voracious on Page 68."

The seriousness with which she critiqued the work garnered my respect and can only be matched by her asking, "Since I know you, Aunt Kathy, and I know that a lot of this story is about your childhood, I think it would be a good idea to let a few of my friends who don't know you read the book and give you their opinion."

"What a great idea, Natalie," I said, as I shook my head incredulously—why didn't I think of that? So, the manuscript was passed from friend to friend, with myriad colored pencils marking places of magic and places of confusion. Natalie punched holes in the overly-loved pages, put the manuscript in a pink leather three-ring binder and mailed it back to me. I had attended writing conferences across the country for years to gain feedback from teachers and publishers. But it wasn't until I sought out the appropriate readership for my manuscript that I began to understand how important it is for writers to go straight to the source. Experts are experts for a very good reason, and teenagers know what they like. Natalie and her cadre of friends distanced themselves from any feelings they may have felt for me, instead going for the jugular, knowing full well that was what they were hired to do. It was that simple for them and that complicated for me. Shortly after incorporating their suggestions, I sent a query to an agent, who asked to see the entire manuscript. Of course, my first phone call was to Natalie.

HARD HAT AREA

Today, we didn't notice the torn wool pants
held at the waist by safety pins that glistened
in the 98 degree temperature or the opened dark
plaid flannel shirt, the under-
shirt Tide white—he could almost be advertising
Abercrombie & Fitch
if it weren't for his shoulder-length matted
brown hair
that cascaded around his mottled face.

We didn't so much notice his rusted grocery
cart
with his broom stuck out of the top like a
hood ornament.
Instead, we saw a construction worker's white
hard hat. It wasn't that it looked so
unusual on him because most things did, but
we wondered instead why he wore it and if we
needed one too.

The Road Home

One year after my family moved to West Virginia, "Howard's New Life," a 1967 episode of *The Andy Griffith Show*, aired on television. The story revolved around the character Howard Sprague's decision to quit his job as county clerk after seeing a travelogue on TV about island life. He sees the opportunity to discover life as a beachcomber in the Caribbean, lying in a hammock all day, enjoying the view and living life on the beach. Ahhhhh.

Howard is convinced that "the grass is greener on the other side," and leaves Mayberry for white sands and blue waters, only to discover that the real treasure in life resides in his own backyard—Mayberry. That structure, familiarity, friends, and fishing holes are his pot of gold.

As a fan of TV Land, I had the chance to see this episode a few months ago. I couldn't help but think it was sent my way not by coincidence, but by some sort of divine provenance, to gently, yet firmly remind me of what I have, I believe, secretly always known—that living in West Virginia is equivalent to that rare discovery of recognizing, before it's too late, that we needn't look any further than our own backyard to find true, genuine happiness.

My family moved from St. Louis to a small town east of Charleston, along Route 60—Charlton Heights. While we initially yearned to "go home," my sisters and I soon found ourselves embracing the thrills of careening from our driveway at the very top of town all the way through town, down the mountain—a swirling distance of about 15 minutes on our Schwinns— the warm summer breeze grazing our cheeks and strands from our long tresses gently stinging our eyes as we landed on the pavement outside the post office and Morrison's Store, where we indulged in Mallo Cups and Smoothies. We seldom had to trek back up the mountain, as most often someone would stop to pick up mail and cart us back home. While we never forgot about the arch outside our bedroom window in the Midwest, its earlier allure and fierce attachment was no match for what was to become an even greater attachment to seemingly endless walks through the woods, sled rides down the mountains, and picnics at Hawks Nest.

And while the nearby city of Montgomery was a bustling thoroughfare upon our arrival, with a business district that boasted restaurants, a movie theater, a department store, furniture stores, and the absolute best G. C. Murphy store in the country (especially for three young girls with limited funds, gleaned primarily from raking the yard after our father cut the grass), its current spirit remains optimistic for the future while the odds are clearly stacked against it. It is that strength of human character mixed with a strong dose of well-defined work ethic that shines brightest in Appalachia and that continues to re-invent itself, becoming the impetus for a continual re-awakening throughout the state.

When my mother passed away suddenly in 2005, I didn't find solace in returning to my birthplace, but instead sought comfort and found peace in Charlton Heights. Several times each week, I would be pulled east, driving from Charleston along Route 60, feeling a sense of renewal and promise the closer I got to my destination. "Almost there" became my mantra, and my sisters would travel vicariously with me, as I called them long distance along the journey, announcing each passing town's name like a train conductor, until my left turn signal clicked and I began my ascent.

As I start the climb up Orchard Avenue and stop for a bit longer each time I visit, closing my eyes and visualizing the floor plan of my childhood home, I am most touched by the recollected sounds of my mother in the kitchen, my father working quietly at his desk, my sisters bustling about, and "walking" through my own room; much of its treasures remain a constant, dependable part of my life (Led Zeppelin's music, favorite reads, and a movie poster from *The Last Picture Show*).

The thick blanket of greenery on both sides of the road, the mountains forming a canopy of protection all around me, and the powerful, almost revered sound of silence brought an "Ahhhh" that assured me that, yes, we can go home again, and in our arriving and tenure we hear the sounds of friends welcoming us back, reminding us that it is in the familiar, the structure, and the rediscovery that we find our pot of gold. In fact, we are comforted by the thought that we never really left it, or perhaps, that it never really left us.

My Thoughts: Relinquishing Beliefs About Race

Kathleen M. Jacobs, Special to The Commercial Appeal
10:02 a.m. CT Nov. 12, 2016

As a child growing up in Memphis in the early '60s, after my parents divorced, my mother hired a strong-willed black woman to watch over me and my two sisters when we came home from school.

Up until that time—as incredulous as it seems now—I had never actually spoken to a black person. In looking back at those times, I believe that lack of communication between "them" and "us" was considered normal—expected and accepted. Now, I realize it was wrong.

Her name was Lila, a very Southern name, a very strong name. I liked it then, and I like it still. But, I would have never told her that I liked her name. I wouldn't have told her then that I liked anything about her.

Like Lila, I too was strong-willed. It seems though that my loyalty to my upbringing was more powerful than the innate knowledge that the way I felt about black people was wrong—destructive to both my strong Catholic upbringing and my self-respect.

But, my childhood beliefs would not be easy to relinquish.

Lila was everything I was certain she didn't deserve to be: compassionate, witty, graceful, and incredibly empathetic. As a child, I thought those qualities had only been gifted to those in my very small world: parents, siblings, friends and my teachers at St. Ann Catholic School in Bartlett. I was, most assuredly, wrong.

Over the few years that I knew Lila, I realized much too late that she was the one who gifted to me all those treasures that she carried in her shirtwaist dress pocket, pulling them out one by one and letting me examine them, like holding a caterpillar for the first time.

Even after one oppressive summer afternoon when I recited a racially degrading chant to her that my aunt had taught me, I knew that what I had delivered hurt her deeply. And watching her stand with such fortitude on the front porch of our house, robbed from me any feeling of superiority, as her grace reduced me to something foreign—self-loathing.

A few years later, when my family moved to West Virginia, I experienced perhaps an even greater sense of injustice, for the source initiated from my mother's reaction after discovering that I had talked with a young black boy from my class on the bus ride home.

His smile reminded me of Lila's, which reminded me of pure, sweet, unadulterated goodness, much like her crisp, homemade fried apple pies. And when my mother delivered an equally damaging chant to me that afternoon, I recall thinking at that moment that I had come full circle.

What Lila felt on an earlier hot afternoon must've matched what I was feeling on that crisp fall day, when the autumn leaves carpeted our back yard, and I knew that my colors had changed, too.

I both shuddered and reveled in my discovery. And like Lila, I walked away in powerful silence.

Dr. Martin Luther King Jr.'s words continue to resound: "It may well be that we will have to repent in this generation. Not merely for the vitriolic words and the violent actions of the bad people, but for the appalling silence and indifference of the good people . . ."

And what ricochets is justice.

FAREWELL, FAYETTEVILLE
By Kathleen M. Jacobs

Farewell peregrine falcons, facing outward, forward, beyond

Aviaries meant to contain, enclose;

Ravenous species

Eager to soar, explore, and

Wield magnificent, graceful

Exactness,

Leaving in their wake perpetual

Longevity.

Farewell peregrine falcons, soaring

Against the backdrop of a

Yielding,

Expansive sky.

Towering above a

Torrent of

Effervescent eddies, swirling with a

Vociferous, yet graceful glide.

Irrepressible and indignant,

Languishing never, but instead persevering,

Lingering, until

Every soul–every living soul–rejoices in undiscovered treasures
beyond the vast horizon.

DOES WHERE YOU WRITE INFLUENCE
WHAT YOU WRITE?

Over the past several years, I have traveled throughout the country, particularly the northeast and the Appalachian region with my husband. He conducts business while I focus on completing a middle-grade novel and writing op-eds for my hometown newspaper, *The Charleston Gazette*. I often find myself feeling like an early nomad, and the challenges of traveling from town to town and city to city fuel my creative endeavors until it becomes a welcomed anticipation to move to the next location to see how that area, culture, and even climate will affect my writing.

In the global economy that has emerged over the past few decades, many writers find themselves writing from wherever they happen to land: airport terminals, subway cars, commuter trains, and any nook they can slip away to on lunch breaks. It's not really a new story. William Faulkner took the same approach in 1930 with the writing of *As I Lay Dying*, which was written over the course of six weeks while working at a power plant from midnight to 4:00 a.m.

While my humble connections with the literary giant begin with our nocturnal nature, it was with a bit of pride that I discovered that we were linked yet again in 1990 when *Appalachian Heritage* published my first short story. I wrote it during my lunch hours from my office at a small law firm in southwest Virginia where I worked as a legal secretary from 4:00 p.m. until midnight. The story was fed by the view outside my single window—a rusted chain link fence that edged a parched lawn, a dilapidated house on its fringes where a murder had recently taken place, yellow police tape circling its structure.

Without the vivid imagery of the disturbing and intoxicating crime scene outside my office window, the writing of "Confinements" may not have been as concrete. More than twenty-five years have passed since that piece was written (and since I've re-read it), and yet that crime scene is as vivid today as it was in 1990.

My final "encounter" with the southern literary genius came many years later and led me to emulate his habit of writing the outline of his novel A Fable with my own adventures, as I outlined my first middle-grade novel on the walls of my studio apartment in midtown. I collected bits of early-morning and after-school conversations from students rushing to and from school every day, their chatter streaming through the opened windows, mixing with the myriad aromas wafting through from the downstairs coffee shop—an addictive combination.

Could Faulkner's work have been written anywhere? Probably. But, the power plant and its environs certainly added to the strength of the work. Did outlining A Fable on the walls of his study provide a certain measure of creativity for the author that he might not have experienced had he written it on a sheet of paper? Again, probably. Similarly, could I have just as effectively written my short story from the kitchen table of my residence? Doubtful. And, had the chatter of middle grade students not reached my ears every morning and every afternoon, would the dialogue in my book have been as genuine? Again, doubtful.

What happens before us as we write a piece is perhaps as important as the place where we actually write the work. As with most achievements, it's a balancing act, in this case of location and imagination. They are as intrinsically linked as pencil and paper.

Location Reads FROM KATHLEEN M. JACOBS

- **HENRY DAVID THOREAU:** *Walden*. In residence for two years, two months, and two days at Concord, Mass., Thoreau looked to the physical world for his masterpiece.

- **EMILY DICKINSON:** Much of her poetry was written during her 20s and 30s behind her upstairs, closed bedroom door at The Homestead in Amherst, Mass.

- **JOAN DIDION:** *The White Album*. This compilation of Didion's reflections and observations of California life in the 1960s is a gold standard for location-based essays.

- **ANNIE DILLARD:** "Total Eclipse." Written in stark detail, this essay describes the personal experience of witnessing a total solar eclipse.

- **DAVID FOSTER WALLACE:** "Consider the Lobster." The author's presence at the Annual Maine Lobster Festival was essential to this controversial essay.

AU
For Shine

Rolling Richlands
besieged by
buttercups and
boulders of limestone.

The last calf born
in a slight valley–
privacy interrupted
by Halogen light.
In seconds she is
upright and on the
road to her final
destination. Even
in her stupidity she
knows this.

Spring lambs already
there, moaning their
displeasure.

And the nurse walks
into the room and
says, "Can you get
me tickets to the
state fair," and the
tree farmer of
the year says,
"I'll get you
backstage passes
if you give me
another shot of morphine."

And Steve, the
farmhand, herds
the cattle to the
west field, with
AU leading.

View from Thurmond is Rich with Artistic Potential

New York City, Philadelphia, Washington (DC), Charlottesville, Cincinnati, Indianapolis, Chicago: each destination a stop on the Amtrak Cardinal's New York City to Chicago route, with numerous stops in between; Thurmond, West Virginia, landing almost dead center.

As the 2017 New River Gorge Winter Writer-in-Residence, I traveled the road from Fayetteville to Thurmond on more than one occasion over the past three months, and each visit further convinced me that, indeed, West Virginia is leaving untapped a prime opportunity to expand its horizons to include this potential mecca for the introduction, development, and unveiling of myriad artistic talents–not limited to its own rich environs, but stretching far beyond its hills and valleys. Superb artistic talents who, most probably, have yet to soak up the majestic Appalachian beauty that gifts not only visual inspiration, but inspiration that comes from listening to the rushing waters of the New and the Gauley, and sampling local fare, to sensing the determination and perseverance that is woven into the very fiber of Appalachians. Painters and musicians, writers and film producers, woodworkers and furniture makers, fiber artists and sculptors, glassmakers and culinary artists. And while West Virginia certainly produces some of the absolute best artisans in each of these artistic realms, imagine how wide our reach would be if we were to explore the possibility of opening up our doors to invite equally-talented artisans from all venues to explore their craft–to experience the far reaches of their respective crafts–in an environment that naturally invites exploration. In fact, it insists upon it.

As I walked across the bridge that runs alongside the Amtrak Depot at Thurmond, I felt the cool fresh breeze, and I looked to the rushing waters below. Their near-translucent hue and their mild ripples that created inviting eddies gifted not only refreshment of mind and spirit, but something else that whispered with a gentle, but very firm, invitation to reach beyond what had been to what could be—to employ that dogged determination that has so defined us in the past to redefine us in the future. To have the courage to "make it happen" now, to not leave it up to the next generation to implement.

As I walked along the brick pavers, reading the history of the town, gazing into the windows of the architecturally-rich buildings that once housed banks and hotels and gathering places, it became crystal clear to me that we aren't exposing and offering and encouraging artists from all directional points to seek this culturally-rich oasis—an oasis that could, with a bit of effort, welcome and sustain and promote not only their efforts but our own, if we but make it happen. Make it happen, now. Seek the funding necessary to revitalize this potentially-rich part of the state, whether on a state or national level or both. Look into it. Can you imagine scores of artists representing a wide interest of creativity arriving at the Thurmond Depot, carrying easels and laptops and looms and musical instruments and cameras and . . . arriving for artistic nourishment, against the backdrop of one of nature's most spectacular settings? Can you imagine chefs preparing local fare, boarders settling in among the music of the New and the Gauley, sounds emanating from passing trains and rafters and mountain climbers and pedestrian foot traffic? Can you imagine? If you can—and I've no doubt that you can—then what's stopping you from hopping aboard and at least trying, at least knowing that you tried to make it happen, now?

SOLSTICE

The blustery early winter morning arrived without provocation. Court Street had yet to be awakened, and as the snow gathered on the front lawn of the courthouse, the bronze statue of the Marquis de Lafayette appeared even more still than at any other season. In the heavy heat and humidity of summer, he seemed to bear the beads of perspiration on his forehead. And in the springtime, pale pink petals from the dogwoods drifted to his crown. In autumn, leaves of golden yellow and deep crimson scattered to his feet. But this morning, if one looked closely, his lips seemed to quiver from the delicate snowflakes that gathered above his solemn glance.

The bulging, worn canvas laundry bag filled the passenger seat of my two-seater, an unlikely companion in the frigid morning. A light dusting of snow gathered on the windshield and then tossed by the chill of the winds as I made my way to the Wash & Fold.

"Good morning," emitted from a voice not unlike notes from the sweet song of a delicate finch. "You're the new writer-in-residence at the Flats this year, aren't you?"

"Oh, good morning," I replied. "Yes, I am."

"Welcome! Before you start your laundry, please join me for a mug of hot tea and a fresh blueberry scone. I just finished reading *Honeysuckle Holiday* last night, and I loved it! Let's talk about Lucy. I'm simply and utterly in love with her," and I followed as if in a trance.

18 September 1995

Dear Ms. Jacobs:

A belated nevertheless sincere thank-you for your kind letter of last June. I stay months behind in dealing with my mail.

I'm not much good at giving advice to the young, but you might wish to pass this thought along to your students:

If you want to write, WRITE. Writing is a craft you can only master by doing. Don't "fall in love" with what you write to the extent that you cannot edit it. You must be to a great degree objective about your work. Good luck and work hard!

Sincerely yours,

Harper Lee

CREDITS

"The Students," originally published in Grab-a-Nickel, Barbour County, WV, Writers Workshop, Spring, 1999.

"Out of the Mouths of Babes," originally published in Writer's Digest, May/June, 2014.

"Hard Hat Area," originally published in Grab-a-Nickel, Barbour County, WV, Writers Workshop, Fall, 1999. Second place winner in the 1999 Poetry Contest.

"The Road Home," originally published in WVLiving, Fall, 2012, "Mountain Made."

"My Thoughts: Relinquishing Beliefs About Race," originally published in The Commercial Appeal, November 12, 2016.

"Farewell, Fayetteville," originally posted and gifted to Lafayette Flats owners Amy McLaughlin and Shawn Means, as my residency as the 2017 New River Gorge Winter Writer-in-Residence came to a close, March 31, 2017.

"Does Where You Write Influence What You Write?" Originally published in The Writer, July, 2014.

"AU," originally published in Grab-a-Nickel, Barbour County, WV, Writers Workshop, Spring, 1999.

"View from Thurmond is Rich with Artistic Potential," originally published in the Charleston Gazette-Mail, April 12, 2017.

Harper Lee's Letter. Personal Collection of Kathleen M. Jacobs.

www.ingramcontent.com/pod-product-compliance
Lightning Source LLC
Chambersburg PA
CBHW051431270326
41933CB00022B/3488